I0815335

An Imprint of Pop!
popbooksonline.com

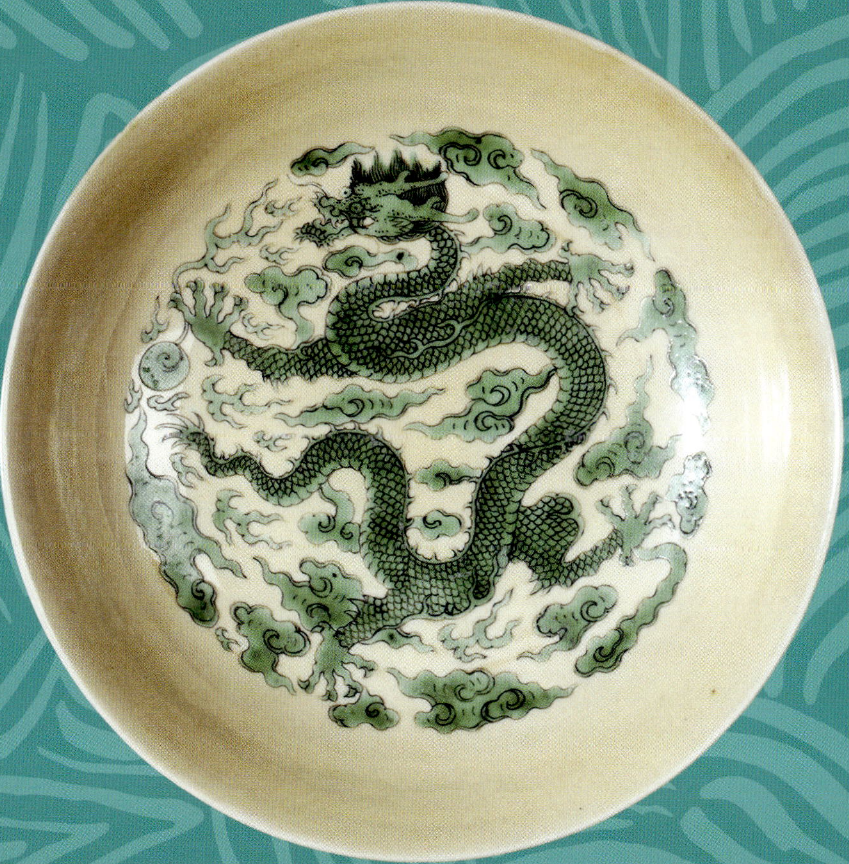

Ancient Mythologies

CHINESE MYTHOLOGY

by Elizabeth Andrews

WELCOME TO DiscoverRoo!

This book is filled with videos, puzzles, games, and more! Scan the QR codes* while you read, or visit the website below to make this book pop.

popbooksonline.com/chinese-myth

abdobooks.com

Published by Pop!, a division of ABDO, PO Box 398166, Minneapolis, Minnesota 55439.

Printed in the United States of America, North Mankato, Minnesota.

102024
012025

Cover Photo: Wikimedia Commons

Interior Photos: Getty Images, Shutterstock Images, Wikimedia Commons, Alamy Stock Photos, Wikimedia Commons/Tokyo National Museum

Editor: Krissy Sterling

Series Designer: Colleen McLaren

Library of Congress Control Number: 2024938591

Publisher's Cataloging-in-Publication Data

Names: Andrews, Elizabeth, author.

Title: Chinese mythology / by Elizabeth Andrews

Description: Minneapolis, Minnesota : Pop!, 2025 | Series: Ancient mythologies | Includes online resources and index

Identifiers: ISBN 9781098247027 (lib. bdg.) | ISBN 9781098247584 (ebook)

Subjects: LCSH: Mythology--Juvenile literature. | Mythology, Chinese--Juvenile literature. | Gods, Chinese--Juvenile literature. | Deities--Juvenile literature. | Mythology, Asian--Juvenile literature.

Classification: DDC 299.511--dc23

*Scanning QR codes requires a web-enabled smart device with a QR code reader app and a camera.

TABLE OF CONTENTS

CHAPTER 1

CHAOS EGG

Before the world as we know it existed, there was nothing but an egg. The egg contained **chaos**. There was a mixture of yin and yang in the egg. Yin and yang are two opposites. They represent the **duality** of life.

WATCH A VIDEO HERE!

Yin is the symbol for women. Yang is the symbol for men.

DID YOU KNOW?

Some yin and yang **concepts** are dark and light, cold and hot, and birth and death.

Pan Gu broke out of the egg. He was a giant. He brought order to the chaos. Pan Gu separated everything into opposites, such as male and female and earth and sky. The earth is the yin. It can be dark and foggy. The sky is the yang. It is clean and clear.

Pan Gu stood in the middle of the earth and sky. His head touched the sky, and his feet touched the earth. The earth and sky

In some myths, Pan Gu has horns and tusks.

The dragon, phoenix, and turtle are important animals in Chinese mythology.

grew. So did Pan Gu. He grew for 18,000 years. At that point, Pan was 30,000 miles (48,280km) tall. The earth and sky were equally as far apart. They would never join again.

Pan Gu's sweat filled rivers. The rivers provided people with water and food.

Pan Gu died. His body created the world. His skull became the top of the sky. His breath turned into the wind and clouds. One of Pan Gu's eyes became the sun and the other became the moon. His hair became the stars.

Pan Gu's body filled the world with living things. His muscles became **fertile** land. Trees and flowers were made from his skin. Pan Gu's body had little bugs living on it. They turned into humans. Pan Gu's sweat became the rain and dew that nurtures all new living things.

Nearly every society has a creation myth. Myths are stories that often involve gods and **supernatural** events. They are not always based in fact. Myths helped people make sense of the world around them.

The sun and moon are opposites like yin and yang.

CHAPTER 2

EMPERORS

Huangdi is the **ancestor** of all Chinese people. He is also known as the Yellow Emperor and the Thunder God. He is the first of the five **divine** emperors that ruled China long ago. When these emperors died, they became gods.

LEARN MORE HERE!

Chinese Cultural Heroes

These **cultural** heroes are gods and rulers who shaped Chinese **civilization** with their inventions and actions. They may or may not have been real rulers.

Three Sovereigns

The three sovereigns invented Chinese society and values. Sovereign is a title given to the highest leaders.

Twins, Fu Xi and Nu Wa

Shennong

Five Emperors

The Five Emperors shaped Chinese culture and served as model rulers.

Huangdi

Zhuanxu

Ku

Yao

Shun

Huangdi was said to have been born in 2704 BCE.

Huangdi was born from the stars nearly five thousand years ago. He could speak right away. During his 300 years of life, he became very wise. As a ruler he was honest. His people loved and trusted him.

Huangdi fought to protect his people. He had the power of nature. Beasts and birds joined his side when he fought. He could even stop the rain from falling and force his enemies into a drought. Huangdi joined all of China together under his rule.

Huangdi created the bow and arrow.

Huangdi also created Chinese civilization. He cut down trees for fire and shelter, made boats, invented clothes, and tamed animals to help people do work. He ordered people to start studying the sun, moon, and stars. Huangdi also created music, writing, and math.

Huangdi's wife was the first person to make silk cloth.

Another divine emperor is Yudi. He is called the Jade Emperor. Yudi rules over all the gods who live in the heavens. He helps them when they disagree. Yudi has guardians that live in Chinese people's homes. They report to Yudi about the people they watch over.

People pray to Yudi for health, safety, and love.

If people live perfect lives, they may become gods or goddesses.

CHAPTER 3

CREATURES OF CHINESE MYTHS

The Chinese zodiac calendar has a repeating 12-year cycle. Each year of the cycle is assigned an animal. Many believe a person has qualities similar to the animal of their birth year. The calendar is based on a Chinese myth.

EXPLORE LINKS HERE!

Chinese Zodiac Animals

Find your birth year!

According to the myth, Emperor Yudi created a way to tell time. He invited all animals on earth to take part in a race. The first 12 animals to win would represent a year. The order in which they

finished is rat, ox, tiger, rabbit, dragon, snake, horse, goat, monkey, rooster, dog, and finally, pig.

RAT AND OX

Animals had to cross a river to finish the race. Rat and Ox reached the river first. But Rat was so tired he couldn't cross by himself. He convinced Ox to give him a ride across the river. When they got to the other side, Rat jumped from Ox's head to finish first!

The Dragon's Body

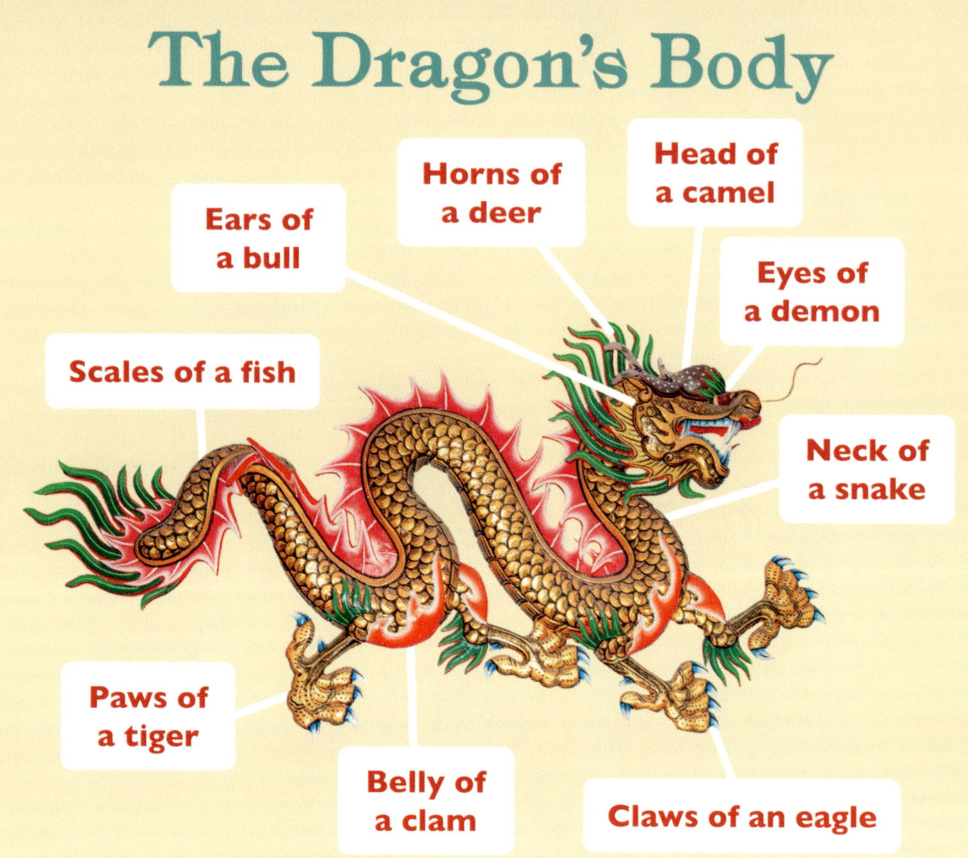

Dragons are very important and powerful creatures in Chinese mythology. They are not evil. Most Chinese dragons don't breathe fire. They are kind and help people.

Some dragons controlled water in lakes, seas, and rivers. Some controlled weather. Dragons could fly, even though they don't have wings. Those that lived in the heavens often used their power to protect villages. Farmers thought dragons were **sacred**. Since they controlled the weather, they could help if a farmer was struggling with his crop.

Dragons appear in many ancient works of art.

A dragon helped Huangdi when he went to war.

CHAPTER 4

WHY IS THE MILKY WAY THERE?

Niu Lang and Zhinu are mythological characters. Niu Lang was a cow herder. His only friend was a talking ox. The ox was once a star in the sky. It told Niu Lang that he needed to keep his hide after he died. The ox hide would carry Niu Lang

COMPLETE AN ACTIVITY HERE!

Oxen were used to plow fields and haul heavy loads. Their hides could be used as fabric.

to heaven. The ox also told him to visit a pond to meet the woman who would be his wife.

Niu Lang and Zhinu the weaver fell in love. But their love was forbidden. Zhinu was a goddess. Her father was Emperor Yudi. He did not want his daughter to be

Zhinu is the goddess of weaving. Weavers make fabric.

with a normal human. Niu Lang didn't know this. He married Zhinu, and they had two children. As time passed, the ox died. Niu Lang kept his hide.

One day, Niu Lang came home and learned Zhinu had been kidnapped and taken back to her home in the heavens. He realized she was a goddess. Niu Lang and his children rode to the stars on the old ox hide. But Zhinu's mother created a river to separate Zhinu from her family.

Zhinu was in charge of weaving clouds in the sky.

The story of Niu Lang and Zhinu explains why the Milky Way is in the sky.

However, when Zhinu's mother saw how sad Niu Lang and the children were, she decided to let the family see each other once a year. Today, people in China honor this story by celebrating it on the seventh day of the seventh month of the year. It is like Valentine's Day in the United States because it honors true love.

The river that Zhinu's mother created appears to humans as the Milky Way in the night sky.

Today, the legends of Chinese mythology can be seen worldwide. The Chinese zodiac still fascinates people.

Dragons are often used in popular art and entertainment. During important festivals, Chinese people put on beautiful dragon dances to celebrate their **culture**.

Dragon dances drive away evil spirits and bring good luck to a community.

MAKING CONNECTIONS

TEXT-TO-SELF

What Chinese animal is connected to your birth year? Do you think you have anything in common with that animal? If not, which animal would you connect with more?

TEXT-TO-TEXT

Have you read about a different ancient mythology? If so, what did it have in common with Chinese mythology?

TEXT-TO-WORLD

Have you ever been to a cultural celebration or festival such as the dragon dance? What was it like? What kinds of celebrations or festivals are part of your culture?

GLOSSARY

ancestor — a family member from an earlier time.

chaos — a state of utter confusion.

civilization — a large group of people who share certain advanced ways of living and working.

concept — a general idea or thought.

culture — the language, customs, ideas, and art of a particular group of people.

divine — relating to gods and goddesses.

duality — the quality of having two different or opposite parts.

fertile — producing plentiful crops.

sacred — something connected with worship of a god.

supernatural — having to do with forces beyond what is natural.

INDEX

This book is filled with videos, puzzles, games, and more! Scan the QR codes* while you read, or visit the website below to make this book pop.

popbooksonline.com/chinese-myth

*Scanning QR codes requires a web-enabled smart device with a QR code reader app and a camera.